POPULAR REPERTOIRE

PIANO
Adventures®
Arranged by Nancy and Randall Faber
THE BASIC PIANO METHOD

CONTENTS

Hedwig's Theme

from *HARRY POTTER AND THE SORCEROR'S STONE*

Key of _____ **Minor**

Music by
John Williams

Misterioso

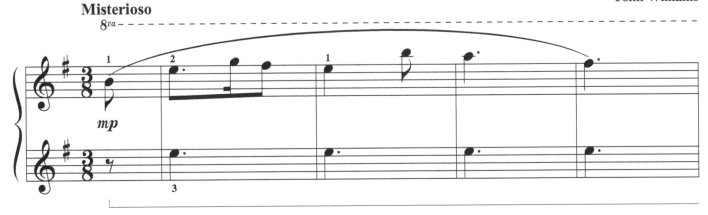

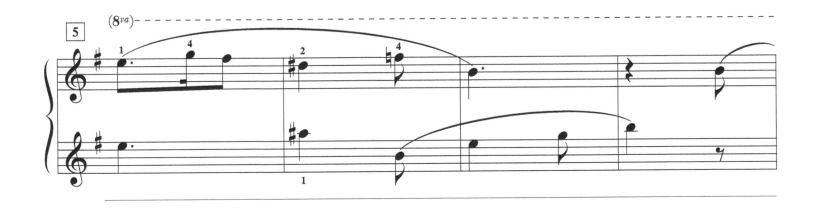

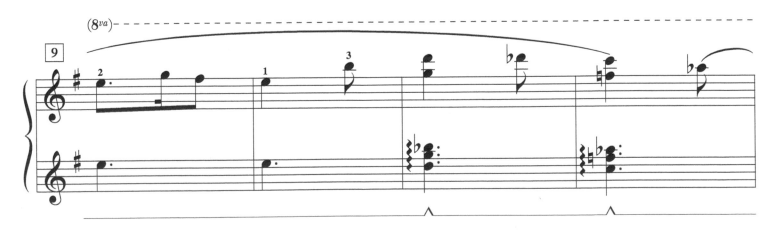

FF1323

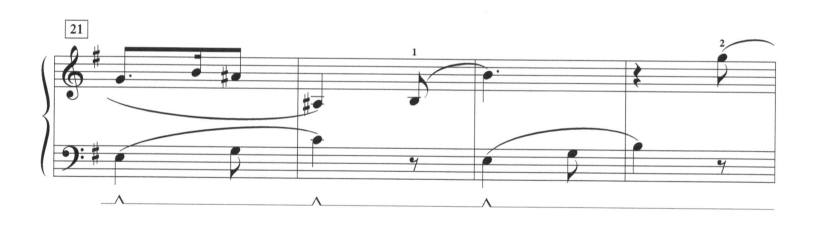

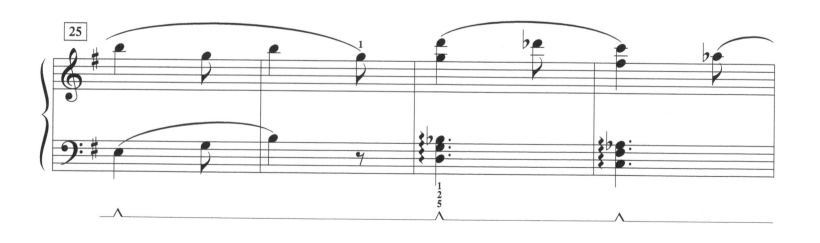

DISCOVERY Are the notes of the ending section (*measure 33* to the end) from the **E natural minor** scale or the **E harmonic minor** scale?

FF1323

Magical Minor Flourishes

To create a showy flourish, the black keys of some scale passages can be taken with the left hand. This is particularly useful with the harmonic minor scale.

Practice these two-hand minor scale flourishes without pedal, then with pedal.

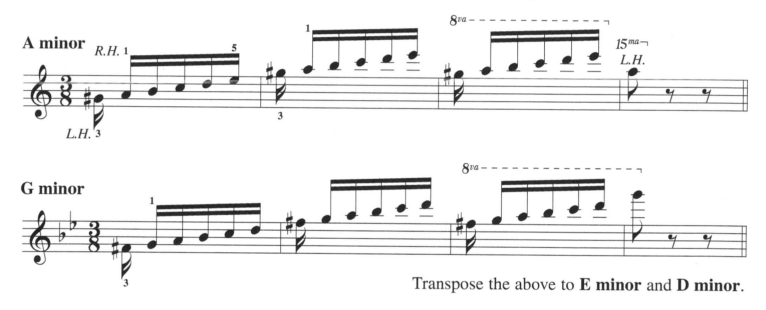

Transpose the above to **E minor** and **D minor**.

Explore shifting to other notes of the scale for a different sound or for ease of playing.

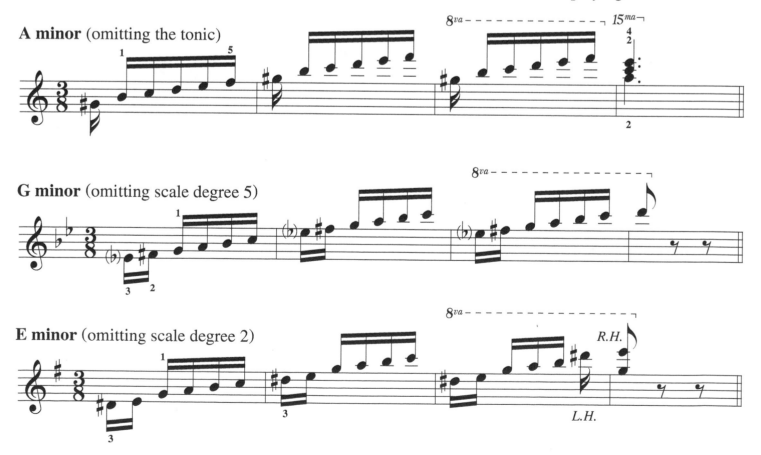

Candle in the Wind

Key of _____ Major

Words and Music by
Elton John and Bernie Taupin

Rather slowly

1. Good - bye, Nor - ma Jean. Though I nev - er
2. *See additional lyrics*

knew you at all, you had the grace to hold your-self while

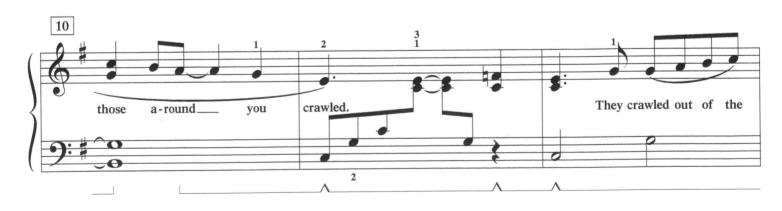

those a-round you crawled. They crawled out of the

FF1323

2. Loneliness was tough, the roughest role you ever played.
Hollywood created a superstar and pain was the price you paid.
And even when you died, oh, the press still hounded you.
All the papers had to say was that Marilyn was found in the nude.
And it seems to me you lived your life like a candle in the wind,...

DISCOVERY Identify the two chords that harmonize *measures 5–20.*
Write the chord name above beat one of each measure.

Chords in the Wind

These are the primary chords
(I, IV, V) in the Key of G:

Each can be played in any inversion.

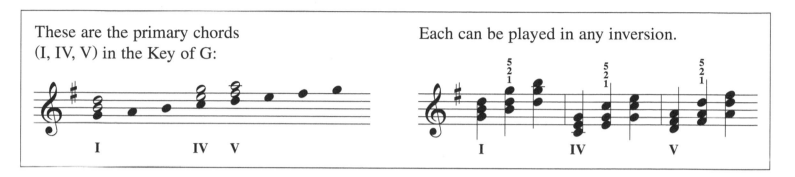

The most common chord change in popular music is the shift between **I** and **IV** chords.

Below is a two-hand accompaniment that alternates between **I** and **IV** chords.
Practice and memorize it using all three R.H. inversions, as shown.

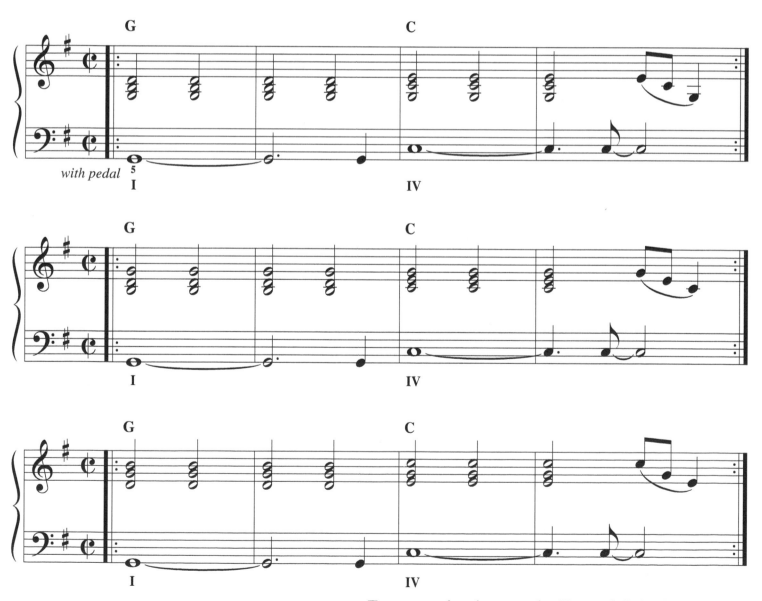

Transpose the above to the Keys of C, D, E, F, and A.

Over the Rainbow

Key of _____ Major

Lyrics by
E.Y. Harburg

Music by
Harold Arlen

Moderately, "in two"

Some - where   o - ver the rain - bow   way   up

high,   there's   a   land that I heard of

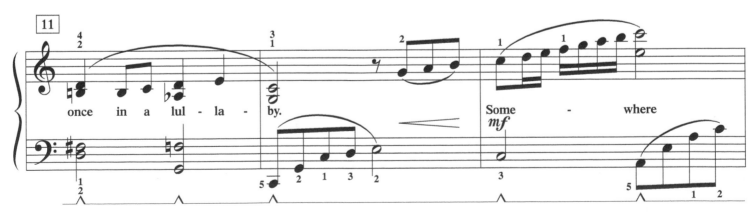

once in a lul - la - by.   Some - where

10

FF1323

DISCOVERY Find three R.H. "fills" that outline a descending **V7** chord (G7).

measures ____, ____, and ____. (Hint: The first note is not a chord tone.)

The End of the Rainbow

Espressivo is the Italian word for playing expressively (with feeling).
To play *espressivo,* observe all **dynamic marks** (including ◁◁ and ▷▷),
tempo marks (e.g., *ritardando*), **slurs**, and **pedal indications**.

Below are alternate *codas* (endings) that replace the last line of music in *Over the Rainbow.*
Practice each, playing *espressivo.* Then choose your favorite ending for use at *measure 43.*

Coda 2

based on music by Harold Arlen

Coda 3

For this ending, write in your own **dynamic marks,**
slurs, **pedal marks**, and *ritardando*.

Coda 4

Summertime

from *Porgy and Bess*®

Key of _____ Minor

By George Gershwin, DuBose and
Dorothy Heyward, and Ira Gershwin

Allegretto semplice

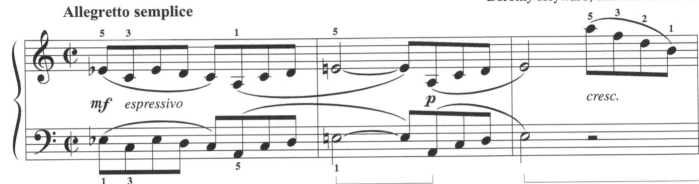

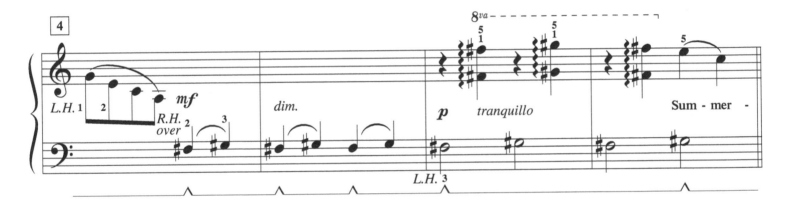

FF1323

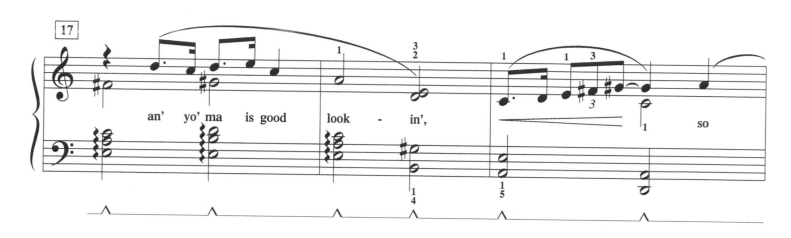

morn - in's_____ you goin' to rise up sing - in',

then you'll spread yo' wings_____

cresc.

an' you'll take the sky.

f But till that morn - in'

there's a noth-in' can   harm   you   with

Dad - dy an' Mam-my   stand - in'   by.

DISCOVERY Look up the following terms in the music dictionary at the back of the book.
Then find each in *Summertime*.

espressivo   tranquillo   poco animato   morendo

Summertime Music Reading

It is important to *really* dig into the score and find what is there.
For every piece you play, study the score for **rhythm**, **harmony**, and **melody**.

A. RHYTHM
• Establish the pulse, then count the passage aloud.
• Do it again, if necessary.

B. HARMONY
• Identify the key, then spot *tonic* (scale step 1) and *dominant* (scale step 5) notes in the score.
• Hunt for familiar chords, particularly **I**, **IV**, and **V**. Play them as written and in other inversions.

C. MELODY
• Look for slurs to identify the melody, then play the melody alone.

For each example, work through steps A, B, and C above.
Then play the passage several times.

Summertime
from *PORGY AND BESS*®

By George Gershwin, DuBose and
Dorothy Heyward, and Ira Gershwin

1. Hint: The F♯ to G♯ inner voice is not part of the melody.

FF1323

2. Hint: The opening phrase is followed by a *transposition* of the same phrase.
Notice the shift of hand position.

3. Hint: Notice the rhythm pattern for each hand.

4. Hint: Notice the R.H. syncopation in *measure 2*.
Write in the counts for this measure.

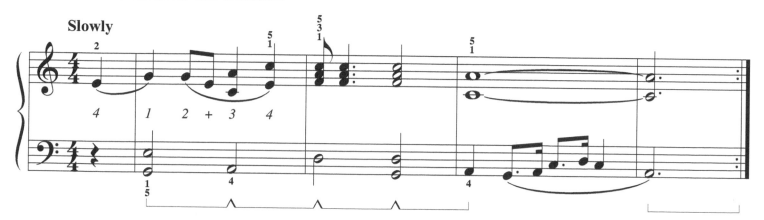

Butterfly Kisses

Key of _____ Major

Words and Music by
Bob Carlisle and Randy Thomas

Rather slowly

Lyrics:

two things I know for sure:___ she was sent here from heav - en, and she's
2. Sweet six - teen___ to - day;___ she's lookin' like her ma - ma a little
3. *See additional lyrics*

Dad-dy's lit - tle girl. As I drop to my knees___ by her bed___ at night,___
more___ ev-'ry day. One part wom - an, the other part girl;___ to

1. There's

FF1323

she talks to Je - sus and I close my eyes. And I thank God for all of the
per-fume and make - up from rib - bons and curls; try - ing her wings out in a

mf

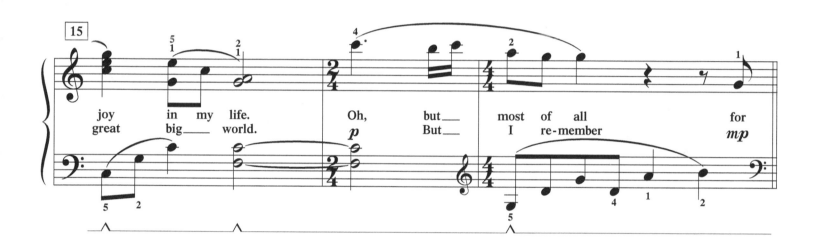

joy in my life. Oh, but most of all for
great big world. But I re-member

p   *mp*

Chorus

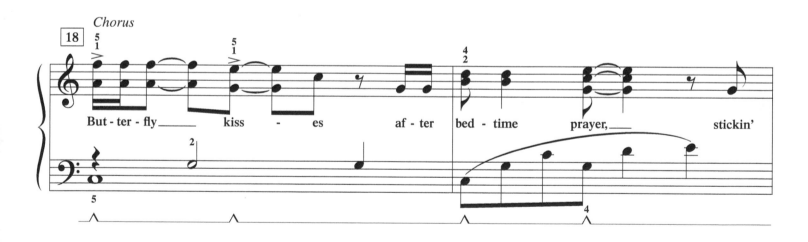

But - ter - fly kiss - es af - ter bed - time prayer, stickin'

lit - tle white flow - ers all up in her hair. "You

"Walk be-side___ the po-ny, Daddy, it's my first ride."___ "I
know how much___ I love you, Daddy, but if you don't mind,___ I'm

know the cake___ looks fun-ny, dad, but I sure tried."___ Oh, with
on-ly gon-na kiss you on the cheek this time."___ }

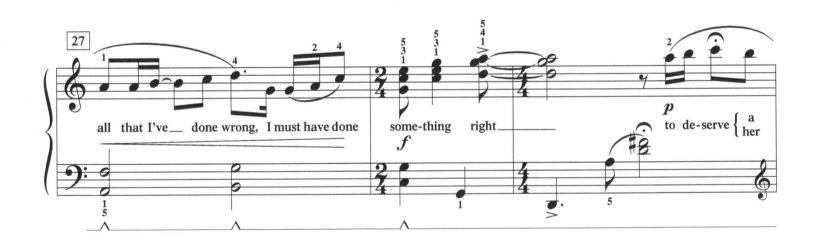

all that I've___ done wrong, I must have done some-thing right___ to de-serve { a her

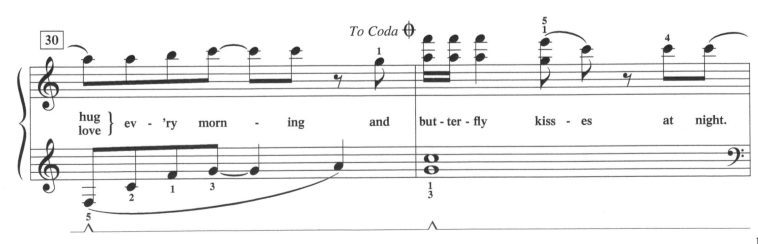

To Coda ⊕

hug } ev-'ry morn-ing and but-ter-fly kiss-es at night.
love }

Verse 3

She'll change her name today;
She'll make a promise and I'll give her away.
Standing in the bride room just staring at her,
She asks me what I'm thinking, and I say, "I'm not sure.
I just feel like I'm losing my baby girl."
Then she leaned over and gave—

Chorus

Butterfly kisses with her mama there,
Stickin' little white flowers all up in her hair.
"Walk me down the aisle, Daddy, it's just about time."
"Does my wedding gown look pretty, Daddy? Daddy, don't cry."
Oh, with all that I've done wrong, I must have done something right
To deserve her hug every morning and butterfly kisses at night.

Write the chord letter names above the staff for *measures 18–28.*

Butterfly Pedal Study

- Write the appropriate chord letter name in the boxes above the staff. Indicate *major* with a capital letter only and *minor* with a lower-case "m." (Ex.: C = C Major; Cm = C minor)

- Play *Butterfly Pedal Study* without pedal, listening to the chord changes.

- Then, draw pedal marks below the bass staff. (⌞‾‾‾‾ ⌃ ‾‾‾‾⌟)
  Indicate a change of pedal where the harmony changes, where your ear detects an inappropriate dissonance, or where the sound becomes too thick.

Butterfly Kisses

Words and Music by
Bob Carlisle and Randy Thomas

There You'll Be

from *PEARL HARBOR*

Key of _____ Major

Words and Music by
Diane Warren

Slowly

mp

1. When I think back on these times____ and the
showed me how it feels____ (to) feel the

dreams we left be-hind,____ I'll be glad 'cause I was blessed to get to
sky with-in my reach.____ And I al-ways will re-mem-ber all to the

have you in my life.____ When I look back on these days, I'll____
strength you gave to me.____ Your love made me make it through. I____

FF1323

look and see your face.
owe so much to you.

You were right there for me.

In my dreams I'll al - ways see you soar a - bove the sky.

In my heart there'll al - ways be a place for you for all my life.

I'll keep a part of you with me. And

ev - 'ry-where I am, there you'll be. And

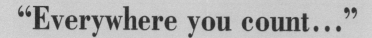

"Everywhere you count..."

16th-Note Patterns

Notice the difference between these two 16th-note patterns.
Tap each several times, counting aloud.

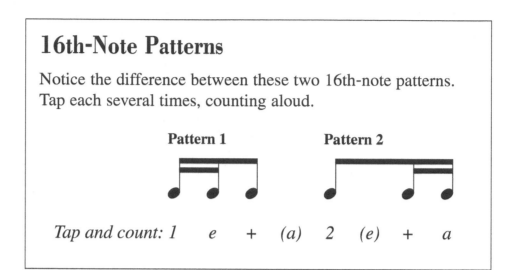

Pattern 1   **Pattern 2**

Tap and count: 1   e   +   (a)   2   (e)   +   a

- Write **1 + 2 + 3 + 4 +** under the melody below to show the rhythm of *There You'll Be.*
  Write the 16th-note subdivision *(1 e + a)* where the melody plays on these inner counts.

- Then play the melody, counting aloud.

There You'll Be
from *PEARL HARBOR*

Words and Music by
Diane Warren

Ex.: + a 1 + 2 e + 3 + 4 + a

(you write)

FF1323

Tears in Heaven

Key of _____ Major

Words and Music by
Will Jennings and Eric Clapton

Moderate, relaxed tempo

1. 3. Would you know   my name_
2. Would you hold   my hand_

if I saw you in heav - en?
if I saw you in heav - en?

Would it be   the same_
Would you help   me stand_

if I saw you in heav-
if I saw you in heav-

FF1323

en?
en?

I must be strong
I'll find my way

and carry on
through night and day

'cause I know
'cause I know

I don't be - long
I just can't stay

here in heav - en.
here in heav - en.

Time can bring you down,   time can bend   your knees.

Time can break the heart, have you beg - gin' please,

beg - gin' please.

Be - yond the door

there's peace, I'm sure__ and I know__ there'll be no more__

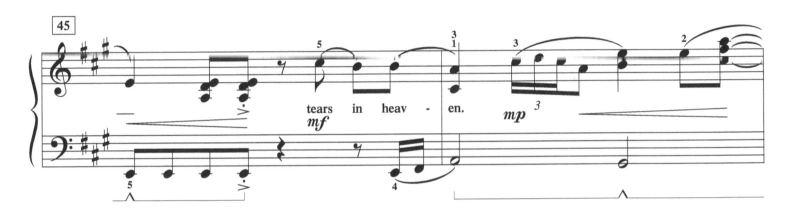

tears in heav - en.

D.S. 𝄉 al Coda

Coda

en.

rit.

Write **1 + 2 + 3 + 4 +** below the R.H. notes for measures 1–4.
Then play the R.H. only, counting aloud.

"Would you know…?"

1. Key

- Name the key for *Tears in Heaven:* _____ Major / minor *(circle)*
- Write the **major scale** for this key, one-octave, *ascending* and *descending.* (Use whole notes.)
- Draw a **sharp** in front of each sharped note.
- Write the R.H. fingering *above* the staff; L.H. fingering *below* the staff.

R.H. fingering:

L.H. fingering:

2. Transposition

Tears in Heaven

Words and Music by
Will Jennings and Eric Clapton

- On which scale degree does the L.H. begin? *scale step* ____
- On which scale degree does the R.H. begin? *scale step* ____
- Play the example, then transpose the first measure down a whole step to G Major.

3. Counting

Write the counts **1 + 2 + 3 + 4 +** for the examples below. Use *e* and *a* for 16th notes, as in *1 e + a.*

FF1323

4. Intervals

Name the R.H. intervals (**2nd**, **3rd**, **4th**, **5th**, **6th**, **7th**, **8ve**).

Ex.: 3rd

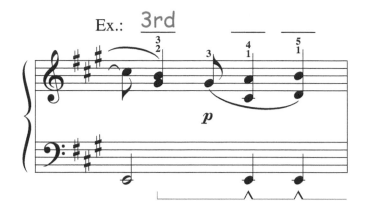

5. Chord Analysis

Write the **chord letter names** in the boxes for this chord progression.
(Remember to include lower-case "m" for *minor.*)

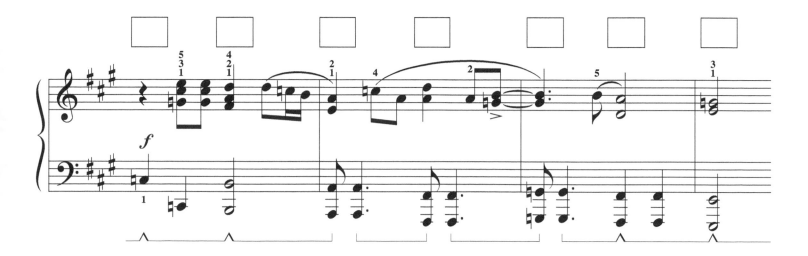

Wind Beneath My Wings

Key of _____ Major

Words and Music by
Larry Henley and Jeff Silbar

FF1323

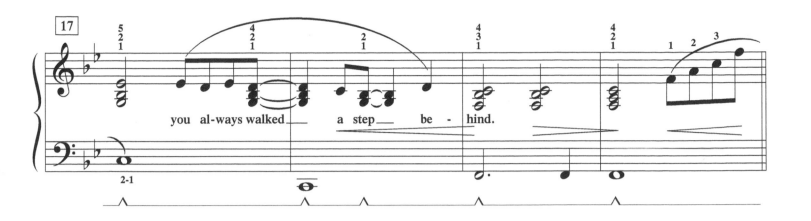

you al-ways walked_____ a step_____ be-hind.

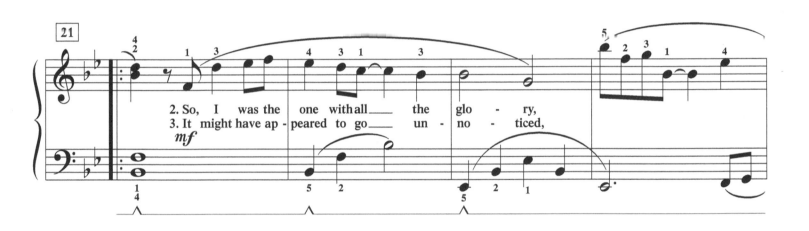

2. So, I was the one with all_____ the glo - ry,
3. It might have ap - peared to go_____ un - no - ticed,

mf

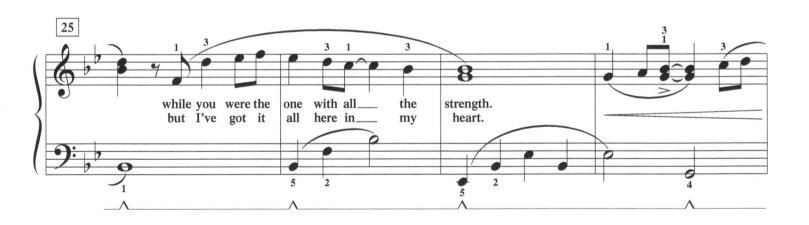

while you were the one with all_____ the strength.
but I've got it all here in_____ my heart.

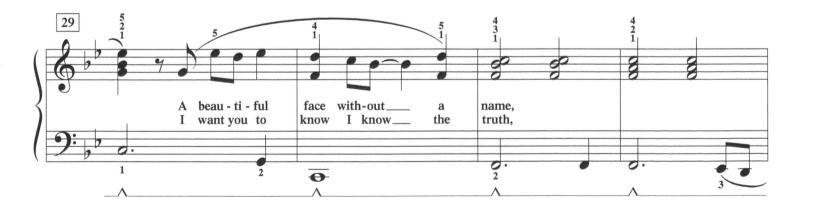

A beau - ti - ful face with-out_____ a name,
I want you to know I know_____ the truth,

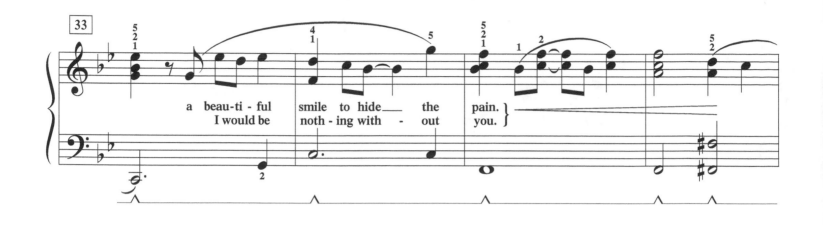

a beau-ti-ful   smile to hide____   the   pain.
I would be   noth-ing with - out   you.

Did you ev - er   know that you're my   he - ro,   *mf*

f

and ev-'ry-thing   I would like to   be?   *mf*

f

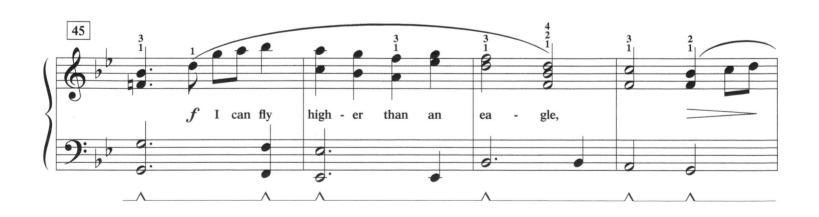

f   I can fly   high - er than an   ea - gle,

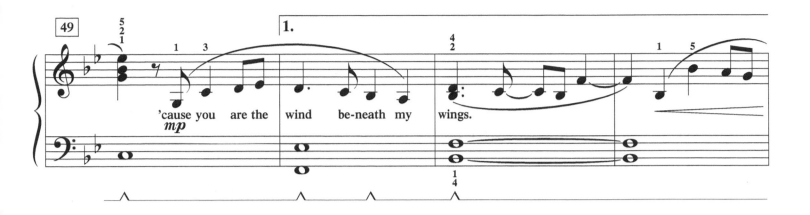

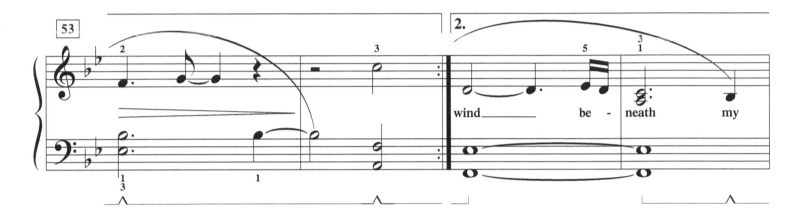

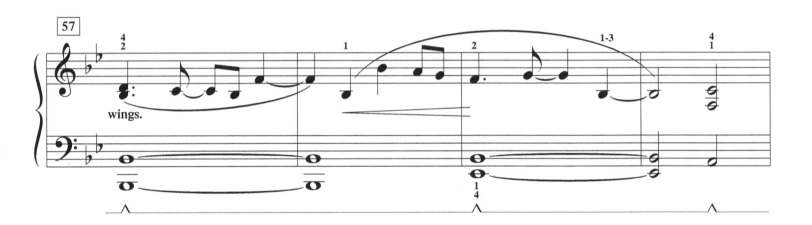

DISCOVERY The first 8 bars of the verse alternate between **I** and **IV** chords (every two measures). Write the chord letter names here, then spot them in the music. **I** = _____ and **IV** = _____

The Bass Beneath My Wings

Wind Beneath My Wings

Words and Music by
Larry Henley and Jeff Silbar

This exercise will help you to hear the bass. The bass is particularly important in popular music because it outlines the chord progression, usually by playing the root and 5th of a chord.

- Your teacher may play either **example a** or **example b**. *Listen* to the bass and determine the example you hear. Then circle *a* or *b*. (The R.H. chords are identical, but the bass notes differ.)

FF1323

- Now sightread each of the examples on the keyboard.
  Notice how each follows the same **I-IV** chord pattern.

Take Five

Key of _____ Minor

By Paul Desmond

Easy swing (♩♩ = ♩³♩)

FF1323

To Coda ⊕

D.S. 𝄋 *al Coda*

Coda

32

35

38

DISCOVERY The chord progression of the chorus *(measure 13)* is based on descending 5ths.

Write the bass notes here: ‖ <u>C</u> - <u>F#</u> - ___ - ___ - ___ - ___ - ___ ‖

Counting in $\frac{5}{4}$ Time

A measure of $\frac{5}{4}$ **time** is usually felt as
3 beats + 2 beats, as in 1 - 2 - 3 - 1 - 2.

- Clap the measure to the right several times,
  noticing the placement of the *accent*.

- Write **1 2 3 4 5** above the beats for each rhythm below.

- Then, tap each rhythm on your lap (or on the closed key cover), counting aloud, **"1 - 2 - 3 - 4 - 5."**
  Feel the accents of the 3 + 2 grouping.
  (Note: R.H. taps the *top* line, L.H. taps the *bottom* line.)

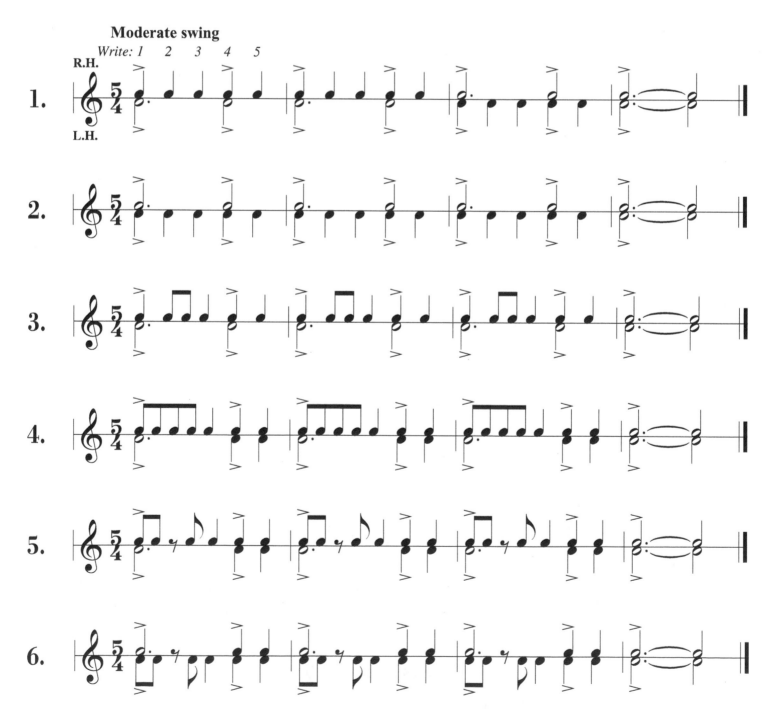

FF1323